BLESSED ARE THE PIECEMAKERS

A Collection of Poems And Uncertain Notions

J. Vincent Hansen

**Illustrated by
Glenn Good Thunder**

North Star Press of St. Cloud, Inc

Back cover art: Mark Coyle

International Standard Book Number: 0-87839-055-3
Library of Congress Card Catalog Number: 89-62675

Printed in the United States of America by Park Press, Incorporated, Waite Park, Minnesota.

Published by:
N̶ **North Star Press of St. Cloud, Inc.**
✝ **P.O. Box 451**
Ṣ **St. Cloud, Minnesota 56302**

To Pappy:
*Who sat with me
on the wall*

and

To Jan:
*For doing what
all the King's horses
and all the King's men
could not.*

Contents

Part II

Part III

They say Vietnam was different but, really, it was like all other wars that came before it, in that it gave so many so much reason to hope for a merciful God.

Part I

Infrared

On
dark nights
allied
with guilt
and
a
Blue Nun,
I
write
eraser poems
on
a
blackboard soul.

Manifest Destiny

Harnessed
to
myth and illusion
like
powerful Percherons
in blinders,
we
ploughed on,
never
looking back
to see the blood
seeping
into
the furrow.

Born 4 July 1947
Died 3 March 1967

War
sniffs
and
nibbles
on
yesterday,
then
takes
its
big bites
out
of
tomorrow.

Pappy

Lured by a screaming eagle
and an ambiguous cause,
you went off
certain of your charge.

Rolled along by fate
and an olive drab myth,
only to find youth
your true adversary.

Silenced in the end
by a faceless foe,
you left us saddened
and asking—why?

When

Vietnam was when
darkness covered the earth
and the oft-sighted light
at the end of the tunnel
was nothing more
than a blazing Buddhist monk.

A Foreign Policy

We turn
    His "Good News"
    into a ledger,
Then put
    our sons
    on the line,
The front line
    to protect
    the bottom line.

1965

In eight short weeks
he went from altar boy to ammo bearer
and in the course of the following year
killed seven people.
It was never so much
that he said yes to murder
as it was that he was unable
to say no to the way it was
in 1965.

Youth

Grant him no quarter,
give him no bone,

Supply him no sling,
provide him no stone,

Cede him no cause,
till he be grown,

For he is half-cocked
by nature alone.

For he is half-cocked
by nature alone.

Caesar

He
is bold and blatant,
as well raw power
can afford to be.
But lo!
He
is subtle too,
like when
he wills
to disconnect a heart
and summons
a barber.

Who?

Sgt. Klein
said: "Wasting
a gook is the
biggest thrill
you'll ever get
with your
pants on."
We
laughed
and
laughed
and laughed.
How we laughed.

Who were we then?

Sgt. Royster Meets Pvt. Stanley

Sgt. Royster said: "Kill the rabbit, Pvt."

Pvt. Stanley replied: "I cannot kill the rabbit, Sgt."

Sgt. Royster repeated: "Kill the rabbit, Pvt."

Pvt. Stanley replied: "I cannot kill the rabbit, Sgt."

Sgt. Royster advised: "I am giving you a direct order, Pvt. Kill the rabbit."

Pvt. Stanley replied: "I will not kill the rabbit, Sgt."

Sgt. Royster persisted: "It would behoove you to kill the rabbit ASAP, Pvt."

Pvt. Stanley replied: "I will not kill the rabbit, Sgt."

Sgt. Royster retorted: "Why won't you kill the damn rabbit, Pvt.?"

Pvt. Stanley replied: "Because it is wrong to kill, Sgt."

Sgt. Royster shouted: "Wrong to kill? Then what in God's name are you doing in this man's army, Pvt.?"

Pvt. Stanley replied: "Nothing in His name, Sgt."

After six months of side sink, Pvt. Stanley was discharged with what was called a personality disorder. (i.e., He would not kill.)

11

Glenn Good Thunder/
Redcatcher/
66-68

A Masquerade

Rifles slung,
laden with ammo,
we went as lovers:

lovers of democracy,
lovers of freedom,
lovers of peace.

We went as lovers:
"parry right and hold" lovers,
"rear take down and strangle" lovers,
"halt, or I'll blow your damn head off" lovers.

Rifles slung,
laden with ammo,
we went as lovers.

Sgt. Karn would begin his class by biting the head off a chicken. Then he would smile and say, "Good morning, men. My name is Sgt. Karn and I'm a Ranger."

Jungle Warfare Training
Phan Rang, South Vietnam

Too Small for Football

Spitting speckled feathers
he said for how
it would behoove us to pay attention,
was going to teach us
how to drive a nose into a brain.

I looked down
at the still pumping Sussex
at his booted feet,
then gazed beyond him
into the green hills
surrounding Phan Rang
and wished for another way
to get Diane Rossman's attention.

Geronimo

The
droning
fades.

Then
mortal
silence
as
we
settle
like
deadly
herbicide
onto
Cong-quack
below.

Little Soldiers

Little soldiers
off they go.

Little soldiers
in a row.

Little soldiers
wound by Ho.

Oh, Lord

Victor Charles, Mr. Two Steps, Delta Don,
Willie Peter, Daisy Cutter, Mama-san.

Widow Maker, Wheeler Dealer, Harlem Hare,
Dragon Lady, Bouncing Betty, Papa Bear.

What a production. What a cast.
Oh, Lord, make it last!

Master Blaster, B.J. Bopper, G.I. Joe,
Jungle Pimp, Hanoi Hannah, Uncle Ho.

P.L. Panther, Jolly Roger, Johnny Reb,
Wrecking Ball, Hyper Sniper, Spider Webb.

What a production. What a cast.
Oh, Lord, make it last!

Oh, Lord, make it last!

Twin Pillars

Fastened
   to twin pillars
   of destiny and death,
blood dripping
   onto
   hard ground below,
he swung
   back and forth,
   back and forth,
   hammock, shroud
   hammock, shroud
   hammock, shroud . . .

The Dark Forest

Propelled
by
doubt and fear
we
advanced
deep
into
the dark forest
leaving
orphans
in
our wake
like bread crumbs
that
we might find
our
way
back again
to
innocence.

Firefight

Rifles
punctuating
for
stuttering
machine guns
so
fluent
in
death.

"Made by Mattell"

He would not go on now
if these was real folks.
Real folks, that is, like he knew
back in Popple Creek.

Folks like Elmer Johnson
and his wife Clara.
Folks like Mat Harper
and his brother Ben.

No, these was not real folks.
These was bogus little folks,
gun-powder gray and rubbery
by the time he got to 'em.

He would not go on now
if these was real folks.
Real folks, that is, like he knew
back in Popple Creek.

Soldiers Never Die Alone

You ask
how long
I've known
soldiers
never
die alone.

I killed
a man
at Pleiku.
When
he died
I died too.

That is when
I first knew,
soldiers
always die
in twos.

These Hands

These hands
clutching
the
blood and betel-stained
Mauser
were good hands.
And while
he laid
forever silent now,
these
thick and tethered-to-earth
hands
yet spoke,
suggesting—
no,
insisting—we would have liked
one another.

The Rainforest

Sometimes
God
allows
the
Devil
to
choreograph
death,
then
sublets
the
rainforest.

Wallowing at Tuy Hoa

It rained
day and night
for thirty-one days
at Tuy Hoa.

We were thankful
for the opportunity
it afforded us
to cry unnoticed.

On Silver Spoons

From
Harvard
he wrote
telling
how
they
had managed
to
fit
fifteen people
into
a phone booth.

From Da Nang
I replied
telling
how
we
had managed
to
fit
seventeen people
into
a helmet.

Sundry Theology

Should someone ask
I will tell them

Vietman was that place
where:

a Hershey bar was worth
   five cigarettes

a pecan nut roll was worth
   five cans of ham and lima beans

a human life was worth
   nothing.

Written after visiting orphanage at Kontum.

Little Folks

Today, I saw
   little folks,
eyes running over with yesterday,
   little folks,
with state-of-the-art scars
behind little doors
all bolted
from the inside now.

Today, I saw
   little folks,
eyes running over with yesterday,
and wondered
   of their tomorrows.

Then You Know Nothing of War

I have been to Bong Son,
    Phan Tiet and Phu Bai.
Now
    when I hear you spew
    your pin-striped 3-piece
    Babbit babbel,
    I say:
Damn your "vested interest."
It is nothing more
than a euphemism
for: brain cells
    dripping
    from a bamboo bridge.

What's that?
Bravado you say?

Then you know nothing of war.

A Bamboo War

hump
hump
hump
hump
hump
hump
hump
hump

hump
hump
hump
hump
hump
hump
hump
hump

hump
hump
hump
BOO!
BAM BAM!
hump
hump
hump
hump

Glenn Good-Thunder
Redcatcher
Co-68

Tyus

We were waving
like canary grass
in autumn wind
when he brought us
the "Good News."
He was precious then
as third cutting alfalfa
in spring.

*Tyus was a barely literate black kid from Alabama who
didn't know much, not much, that is, except right from
wrong.*

You Said God Was on Our Side

You said God was on our side;
I was there and did not see Him.
Which one was He?

Was He the one that triggered the ambush
killing the seven young boys on their way
to school?

Was He the one that raped the already
wounded woman prisoner near
Phan Rang?

Was He the one that shot the panniered
old man crossing a rice paddy, just to sight
his weapon in?

Was He the one that set fire to the
Montagnard granaries in the
Highlands?

Was He the one that dropped the napalm
from thirty thousand feet onto the orphanage
in Kontum?

Was He the one that blew the water
buffalo into the side of a mountain with an
anti-tank weapon "just to have some fun"?

Was He the one strutting with a
Viet Cong ear in a bottle tied
to his lapel?

You said God was on our side;
I was there and did not see Him.
Which one was He?

34

An Old Man and His Chickens

We killed
his chickens,
drank his
rice wine.

We did not
eat his chickens,
just killed
his chickens.

We had brought
our own chicken
in little
green cans.

Once Jesus Had a Cleft Palate

As "number one
shoe shine boy"
snuggled closer
under his poncho,
"numbah one G.I."
wondered:
Who was
this little guy
and what right
had he to tug
in places
long hardened over
like a winter pond?

The Generals

Late at night,
in dim-lit tents
they stick pins
into voodoo maps.

Half-a-world away,
blood spurts out
in little places

like Willow Bend,
Cedar Falls and
Popple Creek.

God, He Must Be Sad

At a side altar
in a dark crypt
she lights a candle;
then prays hard that
her soldier-son might live.

In order that
her soldier-son might live,
he must kill others.

Others,
whose mothers light candles
and pray hard that
their soldier-sons might live.

God, He must be sad.

A Thousand Words of Hate

A thousand
words of hate
employed
to dehumanize
and incite.
A thousand
words of hate
rendered false
by one tattered
telling photo
of a man
with girlfriend
(or maybe wife, I still wonder)
on a blue Vespa.

It Ain't Good, What We Done

Still hitched,
the huge beast
looked down
in bovine awe
at the old man
mangled and moaning
in monsoon mud.

Later that night
on guard
Tyus whispered:
"It ain't good, what we done."

"Snips and Snails and Puppy Dog Tails"

Seven
school-bound
boys
opened
claymore wide,
spread thin
like strawberry jam
onto
a slice
of Asian meadow.
Seven boys
revealing now;
all had lied.
Everyone had lied,
even his mother.

Where Parker Fell

The urbane general
Could not know,

What farm boys guessed
From down below;

That red-clay hill
Where Parker fell,

Was only good
For raising Hell.

Was only good
For raising Hell.

"We Do More before Breakfast . . ."

Inserting
aces
into
cleft
and
cleavage
of
still warm
bodies

A
cock
crows

and
he
wonders . . .

"Yes Sir, Yes Sir, Three Bags Full"

Herman mistook
a team of LRRPs
for a squad of NVA.

Let loose with
40 rounds of duplex
and the LAW.

Moved out to view
his first kills;

one from Arizona,
one from Alabama,
one from North Dakota.

"God is my Pointman, Slackman, RTO, Medic and Ammo Bearer. You know He's hard."
Seen written on a helmet at Kontum

Often Then

We called
on Him often
then.
We had
detoured bad;
no longer
would a
mere Triune God
suffice.

Vietnam

I vaguely remember you calling
something about dominoes falling.
In and out it fades
shadowed by an ace of spades.

Olive drab was in that year
with black pajamas, death and fear.
In and out it fades
shadowed by an ace of spades.

Five days with a prostitute
to deposit what remained of youth.
In and out it fades
shadowed by an ace of spades.

Later at guilt's request
you pinned medals on my chest.
In and out it fades
shadowed by an ace of spades.

When all was said and done
you left me old at twenty-one.
In and out it fades
shadowed by an ace of spades.

Sgt. Major Mack

On a hill
near Phan Tiet,
Sgt. Major Mack
I met.

Three wars
had come and gone
yet Sgt. Major Mack
marched on.

How did
he get so old
and still believe
what he was told?

Did he really
still believe?
Was he really
that naive?

Or instead
might it be said
of Sgt. Major Mack:
one morning
he awoke
too close to a pension
to turn back.

Gonzales

Gonzales had the
Lady of Guadalupe
tatooed on his chest.

Said it was his shield
and he'd be goin' home.

When we loaded him
onto the chopper,
he was smilin' so.

We had to believe
he was home now.

Holy Time

"Hold your fire"
was followed
by holy time in Nam.

Holy time
when the wounded
could be heard
imploring
their respective gods
in gargled tones.

Holy time
when the dead
were poncho-wrapped
and laid side-by-side
like giant cucumbers
in a great garden.

Holy time
when those still whole
would tremble
and ponder,

what if?

The Politicians

12-cylinder words
from
ricksha minds.

Still Life

His taut
brown body
erupted
in a hundred places
like
butterscotch pudding
coming to a boil.
Then he lay
still
as we slithered
back into the
rainforest.

We Take Him Along

This "7 times 70" God,
this "Love your enemy" God,
this "Thou shalt not kill" God,
we take Him along.

Turn Him
from a breaking-bread God
into a breaking-starch God,
from a "turn the other cheek" God,
into a "MAKE MY DAY" God
and take Him along.

Make Him fall in.
Make Him salute.
Make Him march.
Make Him shoot.
This "Thou shalt not kill" God
and take Him along.

Your Left, Your Left,
Your Left, Right, Left.
Your Left, Your Left,
Your Left, Right, Left . . .

Concelebrating

A
golden calf,
in dank fatigues,
one eye on woodline,
sloughing flesh,
paddy pounding,
smoke bringing,
earth scorching,
widow making,
red earth under nails,
body and blood,
7.62 caliber,
leech sucking,
golden calf,
on chest-dried socks,
one eye on woodline,
sloughing flesh,
liturgy.

Upon Entering a Montagnard Hamlet

The things we found
were simple things.
Simple things
    of wood and stone,
        reed and earth.

Neither covered with chrome,
nor could they be plugged in;
we left them,
    strewn and smoldering
        in our wake.

We were Americans first then,
    soldiers second.
Americans first,
on our linear way from Wounded Knee
to only God knows where.

Johnny

Places like Da Nang, Chau Phu,
Duc Pho, Kontum, Pleiku,

Places like the Delta, The
Plain of Reeds, Ashau Valley,
A Street Without Joy,

These places left him
young and hard
like cement
that had set up too soon
in hot summer sun.

Bravado

Unannounced
without resumé smug
he entered
the ward,

certain
even we
had something
left to prove.

Camouflage

He spent a whole semester
    on the Civil War.
Had little blue and gray soldiers
    going round and round
    like wildebeests
    with worms in their brains,
    week after week
    on an old library table
    front and center.
Had smaller battles going
    on windowsills.
Vicksburg
    on an olive drab filing cabinet
    in the corner.
Appomattox on a radiator
    by the window.

A field marshall,
    crew cut, cocksure
    in Roman collar,
    week after week.
Made it panoramic, spectacular,
    BIGGER THAN LIFE!
Had us believing
    there was more to war
    than Cain and Abel,
    more to war
    than grown men peeing on themselves
    at river crossings.

Had us believing
    there was more.

Pappy II

Where are you, Pappy?
I've got good news.
Do you remember, Pappy,
how when we joined in,
we thought they were playing for fun,
then you got that bad deal?
That's what I've come to tell you, Pappy,
you can come back now;
they forgot to cut!

Casualties

We scurried
from the roof
of the embassy.

The "Best and the Brightest"
proclaimed:
"Peace with Honor."

Sometimes in war
words become
casualties too.

Part II

"58,132 killed in action."

U.S. State Department release.

A Tidy List

So
many names
were
missed
on
your tidy list,
when
you
too narrowly defined
survive
and
assumed
all those
who walked away
were
still
alive.

You had a good home and you left, your right.
You had a good home and you left, your right.

On Belonging

To a Squad
    a Platoon
    a Company
To a Batallion
    a Division
    an Army
We were cloaked
rag-lady deep in belonging then.

We had come from different places
to bond in Georgia sun
on dying cockroaches and Jody chant.
From different places
to pull mental slack,
to grow in such a way
so that later
there would always be
someone nearby to say:
"You did the right thing."
"I would have done the same thing."
"Anyone would have done the same thing."

Later
the layers of belonging
fell like veils in a Bedouin tent
and we stood naked and alone.

Naked and alone
we went back
to our different places.

Since Little Elmer Came Back

Nothing gave
Big Elmer more joy
than to hear
Little Elmer sing.
Little Elmer's voice
was rich and healing.
    "More healin',"
Big Elmer declared,
    "than Raleigh salve."

Since Little Elmer
came back, he doesn't
sing any more.

Big Elmer
sure does miss
    "that healin' singin'."

Permanent Issue

From Selma to Saigon,
Montgomery to My Lai,
Willie stored it all up,
layer upon layer
like a ball of sisal twine
wound tight.

Pushed it around
in front of him
like a dung beetle,
until one day someone
mentioned the odor.

Then, facing those
he hated, Willie BLEW
like a claymore mine,
backblast taking out
all those he loved.

Glenn Good Thunder
Redcatcher
66-68

Chief

Many moons ago
in a distant land
of pannier and pagoda,
he left footprints.

Now the Great Spirit
tracks him
like a wounded elk
in fresh winter snow.

Pallbearers

While
sights and sounds
are content
on occasion
to pry and prick,
smells
are the
pestering pallbearers
of war,
determined
to march on
with no intention
of ever
lowering the casket.

Bernard

He had duct-taped
her best paring knife
to the barrel
of his BB gun.
From an upstairs window
she watched
as he gleefully stabbed
the small red sparrow
again and again.

Years later,
when the taller soldier
handed her the telegram,
she tried to recall
when it was
he really died.

"As You Were"

Floyd is happily
married now.
Works in a bank;
sells Ginnie Maes
and IRAs,
sings in the choir,
ALWAYS votes,
sometimes writes
a letter to the editor.

Says
the only thing
that bothers him
about the Nam,
is that
it doesn't bother him.

An Elusive DEROS

He told them
about the gray
squirrel throwing
the grenade.

They laughed
so hard
at him then.

He will not
tell them about
the woodchuck
in black pajamas.

DEROS: Date of Expected Return from Overseas

Overkill

Danny says he was headed
for trouble before the Nam
came along.

Danny says he wasted
three gooks in the Nam.

Danny says the Nam was
good for him: helped
him become a man.

Danny says he hopes
another Nam comes along
for his two sons.

Danny says he was headed
for trouble before the Nam
came along.

No Payments till April

One side of his helmet read:
"Avoid Jetlag; Go Body Bag."
The other: "Death Spoken Here."
We skirted him like a farmer
does a slough-hole.
 Wrecking Ball was hard,
 wrecking ball hard.
Two tours on the line.
Ask anybody and they'll tell ya:
guys who put two tours on the line,
were fewer than vegetarians
who pray the rosary.
 Wrecking Ball was hard,
 wrecking ball hard.
Back home,
he never talked Nam.
Not even his Ma noticed
when he stopped using
the future tense.
 Wrecking Ball was hard,
 wrecking ball hard.
It was late October
when his Pa found him hanging
in the box elder grove
behind the granary
and wondered . . .

who would do the spring plowin'?

A Shallow Grave

After the Nam,
Leo became a
pacifist,

went all around
talking against
the war,

named his sons
Phillip and Daniel,

then almost took his
wife's damn head off
when she forgot to
put moth balls in
with his uniform.

Roosting at the V.F.W.

Day after day.
Night after night.
Bottle after battle.

His life now
a race between
liver and soul.

Glenn Good-Thunder/
Redcatcher/
66-68

Earl

Earl killed four Viet Cong
at Tuy Hoa on August 16, 1966.

Earl killed a 14-point buck
at Duluth on October 22, 1971.

Earl killed himself at home
on April 7, 1979.

*Like a usurping uncle, Vietnam picked Earl up, tossed
him into the air—then disappeared.*

Rosie and Herman
(A soldier's soldier)

If they go
to the evening Mass,

If they sit
in the back pew,

If they leave
after communion,

Perhaps no one will notice
the black and gun-metal blue eye.

Despair

Not
in dwelling
on what
he did
in Vietnam,
does he
become
most intimate
with despair;
but rather
in the
realization
that he
is capable
of doing it
again.

Glenn Good-Thunder
Redcatcher
66-68

Part III

Part III

Uncertain Notions

How
I long
for that time
when
right and wrong
and truth
were mine.
That day
before
black and white
gave way
to gray
and left me
with
uncertain notions
only.

Hindsight

They said:
join us
and see
the world's
sights.

They did
not say
join us
and see
the world
through sights.

Glenn Good-Thunder
Redcatcher
66-68

That's What I'm Thinkin', Pa

Finally, Big Elmer ventured:
"What'cha thinkin', Little Elmer?"
"Know what I'm thinkin', Pa?"
"No, son. What'cha thinkin'?"
"I'm thinkin' maybe we got it wrong, Pa.
I'm thinkin', maybe God intended
for cows to be soldiers
and that's why
He giv'em four stomachs.
That's what I'm thinkin', Pa."

With No Lions to Kill

When he was seven
he fell in love with a girl
with freckles on her nose
and auburn hair.
He brought her tadpoles
in a Mason jar,
belly-up and bobbing
in the mid-day sun.

When he was twelve
he fell in love with a girl
with dimples
and a pony-tail.
He trapped gophers
all that summer
and bought her a necklace
in the fall.

When he was seventeen
he fell in love with a girl
with lips
and breasts.
He killed gooks
all that year
and bought her a diamond
in the spring.

Pappy III

They are saying
you were brave, Pappy,
that what we did was good.
When I say
you were not brave, Pappy,
that what we did was not good,
they do not understand.

But you understand,
don't you, Pappy?

If I let them say
you were brave,
that what we did was good,
they will use
their memory of you
to kill again and again.

That is why
I cannot let them say
you were brave,
that what we did was good.
Don't you see, Pappy?
I know no other way
to give meaning to your death.

Superpowers

Superpowers
   never like
to entertain at home.
   They like
to be invited out
   by the Koreas,
   El Salvadors,
   Afghanistans
   and
   Vietnams.

They know,
   I suppose,
how hard it can be
   on the furniture
   and too
   how it keeps the children up
even long after
   it is over.

The Systematic Reduction of Enemy Cadre
                              Army euphemism for killing

Bad Semantics (B.S.)

So hygenic, so stainless,
So innocent, so painless.

No blood, no gore,
No feces on the Huey floor.

No endless rows of
Charred bodies to dispose of.

As if it could all be done
in the living room, without
setting off the smoke alarm.

Hate

Naked
he sires
little words
like
gook, kike
and *spik.*
Then
puts on
his
uniform
and
gives birth
to
big words
like
holocaust and
genocide.

Soldiers

Soldiers always
make orphans

Then go
to an orphanage

Hand out
candy and gum

Then go home
feeling good inside.

Americans

A lot of folks
in Asia don't
like us now.

We cannot
understand
why.

We are like the boy
who killed his parents,
then asked the court to
go easy on him because
he was an orphan.

Patriotism

A
>> once proud eagle
>> soaring high
> on
clouds of truth and honor,

dazed and tattered now,
>> hovering
>> over death
like a Serengeti buzzard.

On Killing

Kill a man
charging and it
may well be the last
you see of him.

Kill a man
fleeing and he
will likely settle
in your neighborhood.

Kill a man
sauntering and he
will take up residence
in your soul.

A Pinch of Salt

To
    lethal lieutenants,
    ambitious captains
    and mad majors,
I add
    callous colonels,
    gung-ho generals,
    hard-boiled sergeants
    and cocksure privates.
I mix in
    a duce-and-a-half
        of pre-sweetened Kool-Aid,
    some wait-a-minute vines,
    some betel nuts,
    some rice wine
    and a small nun
        with a Baltimore Catechism.

I stir and stir and stir.

The poems
    always set up confessional.

Donahue, Dow Jones and Disneyland

The pain
keeps him now
in this
hallowed place
of pond and popple.
Not
the 2-aspirin pain
that came
from having killed,
but the
whole-bottle pain
that came
when reminded
of what he had
killed for.

Rip Van Winkle

Twenty years later
he still says, "The politicians tied
    our hands!"
  Still says, "If only they had
    let us go into
    the north!"
  Still says, "If only we had
    bombed the harbor
    in Haiphong!"
  Still says, "We could have
    won that war!"

Twenty years later,
still says these things—

As if time were a eunuch.

On Jesus, Jack Pine and Praying Mantes

They say Jesus died
in order that we
might have life.

They say the fire
in which the old Jack Pine dies,
gives birth to the seedling.

They say after
Praying Mantes mate,
the female devours the male.

Soldiers,
especially soldiers,
must view these lives;
these lives of Jesus,
Jack Pine and Praying Mantes.

". . . This You Do unto Me."

After
you kill Jesus,
Christmas
becomes something different.

After
you kill Jesus,
Christmas and Good Friday
become one.

After
you kill Jesus,
you back up into October,
then, running hard,
you try to leap
from November to January.

After
you kill Jesus,
Easter stays distant;
out of reach,
like top shelf candy.

Guilt

Through
a crack
in the wall
I
observe
medals,
ribbons
and
fourragere
dousing
smoldering
guilt
in a clearing
near
my
soul.

The Wall

To what avail
this palling wall
constructed to recall
those who lost
their lives
while
taking lives?
To what avail
this palling wall?

Tell Me, Soldier, Is It So?

It is rumored
you can no longer
    smell flowers,
    behold butterflies,
    hear geese in autumn flight,
    nor cry when your brother dies.
Tell me, soldier,
    is it so?
I must know
    before I go.
So tell me, soldier,
    is it so?

Our Poems

Suckled
on
Freud and Dewey,

we know
not
sin.

Reebok bound
for
heaven,

only
our poems
expose us.

Alchemy

I
hear
them say
the whole
was noble
and
wonder
where
it is
they have
stashed
so many
of
the little
pieces.

Always

Rain always
 reminds me of monsoons.
Monsoons always
 remind me of mud.
Mud always
 reminds me of the jungle.
The jungle always
 reminds me of bamboo.
Bamboo always
 reminds me of fishing.
Fishing always
 reminds me of leeches.
Leeches always
 remind me of blood.
Blood always
 reminds me of the Nam.
The Nam always
 reminds me of rain.

Standing Guard

On
Goodyear rubber
they advance,
Aspersion and Innuendo,
point and slack
for
Caesar
in the middle of the night.

I dare not doze.

War

I
have seen
her
naked
now
and
will
not
trust
streetlamps
again.

The Enemy

This thing
 that burns in me,
This thing
 that takes the lives
 of mallards and men,
This thing
 that leaves love
 charred and smoldering
 in its wake,
This thing
 is like a trick candle
 that will not stay out.

To Lenny and Simon

They will say:
    you should be
    willing to die
    for your country.
They will not say:
    you should be
    willing to kill
    for your country.
But always remember:
    you will never
    have to live
    with having died.

Blessed Are the Piecemakers

Some time
has passed
and now
a frail old woman
quilting
quietly,
gives him more hope
than
all the world's
armies.

Family Tree

In
quest
of shade
below
the
lowest limbs
we stayed.
Perchance
had
we perched
on
a higher branch,
we might
have seen
we were
brothers.

Glossary

Ace of spades - An ace of spades was placed on the bodies of slain enemy soldiers as part of psychological warfare.

ASAP - As Soon As Possible

Claymore mine - A mine commonly used by the infantry in Vietnam for perimeter defense.

Dying cockroach - Slang for a calisthenic commonly employed in military training in which a soldier lays flat on his back with his feet extended into the air

Duce-and-a-half - Slang for a military truck with two and a half ton capacity.

Huey - A helicopter.

Hump - To walk with backpack.

Jody chant - Chant used while running in training.

LAW - Light Anti-tank Weapon

LRRP - Long Range Reconnaissance Patrol

NVA - North Vietnamese Army

Point - First man in a column.

RTO - Radio and Telephone Operator

Side sink - KP duty of worst kind: pots and pans.

Slack - Second man in a column.

Vespa - Italian motorscooter.

Wait-a-minute vines - Any vine that soldiers would catch on in the jungle.